5 APR 1995

MSC

ROTHERHAM PUBLIC LIBRARIES

This book must be returned by the date specified at the time of issue as the Date Due for Return.
The loan may be extended (personally, by post or telephone) for a further period, if the book is not required by another reader, by quoting the above number   **LM1 (C)**

A TASTE OF SPAIN

Bob Goodwin and Candi Perez

Wayland

Titles in this series

A TASTE OF

Britain	Italy
The Caribbean	Japan
China	Mexico
France	Spain
India	West Africa

Cover *Olive groves in Andalusia.*

Frontispiece *The Alcazar, or palace, in Segovia, built during the Middle Ages.*

Editor: Joanne Jessop
Designer: Jean Wheeler

First published in 1994 by
Wayland (Publishers) Ltd
61 Western Road, Hove
East Sussex, BN3 1JD, England

© Copyright 1994 Wayland (Publishers) Ltd

British Library Cataloguing in Publication Data
Perez, Candi
Taste of Spain. – (Food Around the World
Series)
I. Title II. Goodwin, Bob III. Stevens,
Judy IV. Series
641.300946

ISBN 0–7502–1208–x

Typeset by Dorchester Typesetting Group Ltd
Printed and bound by Lego, Italy

Contents

Spain and its people

The land

Spain is the second largest country in Europe and occupies an area of land known as the Iberian Peninsula. The northern coast faces the Atlantic Ocean and the Bay of Biscay. The Pyrenees mountain range runs along the northern border between Spain and France. To the east and south is the Mediterranean Sea. At the southern tip of Spain is the British military base of Gibraltar, which overlooks the narrow Strait of Gibraltar

A mountain village in southern Spain. Gibraltar and North Africa are on the horizon.

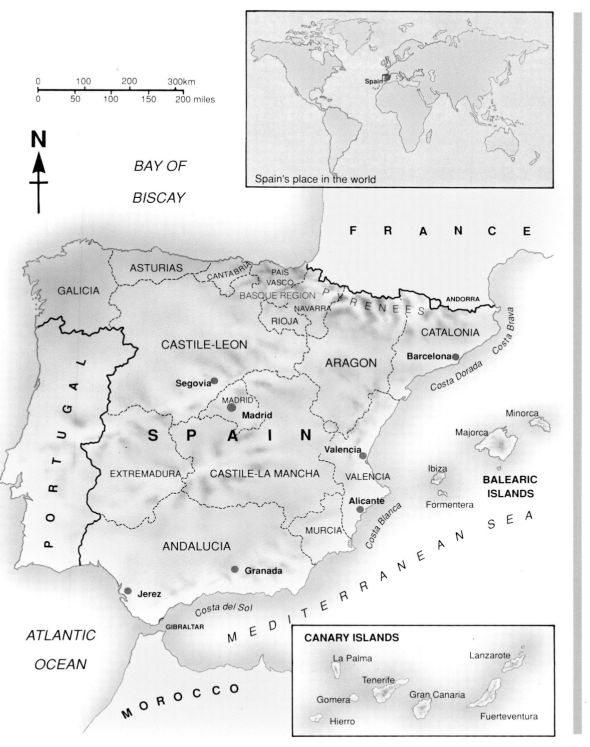

Spain's place in the world

N

BAY OF

BISCAY

0 100 200 300km

0 50 100 150 200 miles

FRANCE

GALICIA

ASTURIAS

CANTABRIA

PAIS VASCO

BASQUE REGION

NAVARRA

RIOJA

PYRENEES

ANDORRA

CATALONIA

CASTILE-LEON

ARAGON

Barcelona

Costa Brava

Costa Dorada

Segovia

MADRID

Madrid

S P A I N

Valencia

Minorca

Majorca

BALEARIC
ISLANDS

P O R T U G A L

EXTREMADURA

CASTILE-LA MANCHA

VALENCIA

Alicante

Ibiza

Formentera

Costa Blanca

MURCIA

ANDALUCIA

Granada

M E D I T E R R A N E A N   S E A

Jerez

Costa del Sol

GIBRALTAR

ATLANTIC

OCEAN

M O R O C C O

CANARY ISLANDS

La Palma

Tenerife

Gomera

Hierro

Gran Canaria

Lanzarote

Fuerteventura

5

A taste of Spain

These windmills, and the castle in the background, are in central Spain.

between the Mediterranean Sea and the Atlantic Ocean. To the west of the country is Portugal. The Balearic Islands in the Mediterranean and the Canary Islands, 1,200 kilometres south-west in the Atlantic off the coast of Africa, also belong to Spain.

Mainland Spain is divided into seventeen regions, which all have quite different customs and traditions. The things that people usually think of as typically Spanish come from the region of Andalusia, in the far south. This is the home of guitars and flamenco dancing. The well-known tourist area Costa del Sol is in Andalusia as well.

The people

Spain has a population of about 40 million people. In the past, most Spaniards made a living working on small farms. However, in the last fifteen years, more and more people have left the countryside to work in the towns and cities. Today many Spaniards live in cities, and some of the old villages are like ghost towns.

The Spanish are famous for their flamenco dancing. This exciting and complicated dance is usually accompanied by guitar music, while the audience claps out the rhythm.

The languages of Spain

Almost all Spaniards speak Castilian, which is usually referred to as Spanish. But there are three other languages that are also spoken in Spain.

In Galicia in the north-west, the people speak Galician, which is similar

Above *A small village in the Basque country.*

Below *A harbour inlet in Minorca, one of the Balearic Islands.*

to Portuguese. The Galicians are descended from the Celts, an ancient people from western Europe.

At the western end of the Pyrenees is the Basque country where the people speak the Basque language. Some people think that the Basques were the first people to live in Europe, thousands of years ago. The Basque language is completely different from all other languages and is very complicated.

At the eastern end of the Pyrenees is Catalonia where the people speak Catalan, which is like a mixture of Spanish, French and Italian. In Valencia and the Balearic Islands some people speak a dialect of Catalan.

History

The aqueduct at Segovia is one of more than two hundred aqueducts built by the Romans when Spain was part of the Roman Empire. These stone water-ways brought fresh water from springs that were often many kilometres away.

Throughout its history, Spain has been invaded and conquered many times. The first people to conquer the whole of Spain were the Romans, in 204 BC. The Romans built long straight roads and an irrigation system to bring water to dry areas of the country. Some Roman aqueducts are still standing today, such as the one at Segovia.

The Romans ruled Spain for five hundred years, until they were defeated by the Visigoths, who ruled for the next

Above *The Allhambra is a magnificent palace built for the Muslim rulers in the thirteenth century.*

Below *This statue in Granada shows Columbus reporting his discoveries to Queen Isabella.*

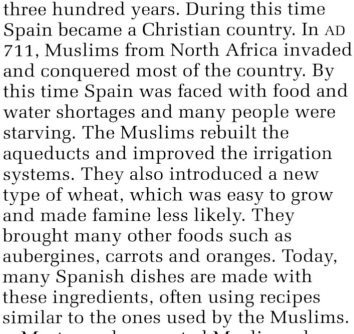

three hundred years. During this time Spain became a Christian country. In AD 711, Muslims from North Africa invaded and conquered most of the country. By this time Spain was faced with food and water shortages and many people were starving. The Muslims rebuilt the aqueducts and improved the irrigation systems. They also introduced a new type of wheat, which was easy to grow and made famine less likely. They brought many other foods such as aubergines, carrots and oranges. Today, many Spanish dishes are made with these ingredients, often using recipes similar to the ones used by the Muslims.

Most people accepted Muslim rule, but some groups of Christians continued to fight against the Muslims for the next eight hundred years. They finally recaptured Spain from the Muslims in 1492. That same year Christopher Columbus, supported by the king and queen of Spain, set out on his voyage around the world and arrived at what is now known as the Americas.

The sixteenth century is considered the Golden Age of Spain. During that time, Spain was the most powerful and important country in Europe and had established a vast empire that included most of South America and parts of North America.

Spanish explorers in the New World brought back many foods, such as maize, tomatoes and potatoes, that were new to Europeans.

By the beginning of the nineteenth century, Spain was less powerful and the Spanish Empire began to fall apart. Between 1936 and 1939 there was a civil war in Spain. General Francisco Franco and his followers won the war and Franco ruled the country as a dictator. In 1975, when Franco died, Prince Juan Carlos was crowned king of Spain. He is very popular with Spaniards because he decided that Spain should have a democratic government. The first free elections were held in 1977.

Today, Spain is an important member of the European Community, which it joined in 1986. It has been host to football's World Cup, the 1992 Olympic Games and the World Trade Fair (Expo '92). In 1992, Madrid, the capital city, was named European City of Culture.

Madrid, with a population of over 3.5 million, is an exciting and beautiful city in the heart of Spain.

Food production

Farming

The types of farming in Spain vary greatly because of the differences in climate throughout the country. The north is wet, and the south is very dry. Much of the centre of Spain is a high, flat plain known as the Meseta. Here it is cold in winter and extremely hot in the summer. The Meseta is a dry area, and the main crops are wheat and maize. Farmers also raise sheep and goats. Hundreds of years ago, farmers of the Meseta used to gather enormous flocks of sheep, which they herded around Spain like cattle in a Hollywood Western. Although the huge flocks are gone, there are still plenty of sheep in the Meseta.

A shepherd of the Meseta, the high, flat plain in central Spain, with his flock of sheep.

In the wetter northern regions, farmers grow fruits such as apples, pears, plums, peaches, melons and figs. In the southern areas pomegranates, avocados and citrus fruits are grown. Marmalade, a traditional English jam, is made with oranges from Seville, the capital of Andalusia. Valencia is another area

An orange plantation near Seville.

13

A taste of Spain

Planting rice in Valencia, where there is plenty of water to irrigate the rice fields.

Blossoming almond trees.

where oranges are grown. Rice is also grown here because there is plenty of water for irrigation.

Spain is generally too hot to produce many dairy products. However, in the north-west, where the climate is cooler than in the rest of the country and heavy rainfalls produce lush pastures, there are some dairy farms.

The mild climate in the Canary Islands is ideal for farming, but the land is hilly. To solve the problem, farmers have built stone terraces filled with

Steep terraced fields on the Canary Islands.

earth brought in from elsewhere. The main crops are bananas and tomatoes, many of which are exported.

Almonds are grown in the south and in the Balearic Islands. Almond trees in blossom are a beautiful sight in the springtime.

Spain is one of the world's largest producers of olives and olive oil. Olives are grown all over the country. In parts of Extremadura and Andalusia the olive groves stretch as far as the eye can see. The trees are neatly arranged so that

15

A taste of Spain

Above left *These olive groves in Andalusia stretch as far as the eye can see.*

Above right *A typical countryside scene with huge olive trees and wild flowers.*

trucks and harvesting machines can be used. Even in Roman times, olives and olive oil were exported to Britain. Recently, archaeologists found some two-thousand-year-old Spanish olives at the bottom of the River Thames.

The owners of most small farms have a few olive trees and almond trees, but they make very little money from these crops so they generally keep them to eat themselves.

Wine

The Spanish have been growing grapes and making wine for thousands of years. Many farmers harvest a few grapes each year to make their own wine. Often a group of farmers in a particular village collect all their produce together. These groups are called co-operatives. By working together, farmers can share the cost of expensive machinery to make their farms more efficient.

Picking grapes in Valencia; the grapes will be used to make wine.

Above *This man is sampling some hundred-year-old sherry.*

Below *A vineyard in La Rioja region.*

In some areas wine is big business. Sherry, the most famous Spanish wine, comes from the area around Jerez. The English had difficulty pronouncing Jerez correctly, so they called it 'sherry'. Sherry became such a popular drink among the English that some English people moved to Spain to produce sherry. Today, many of the Spanish families that make sherry have English ancestors and English surnames.

Wine from the La Rioja region has always been famous in Spain and is now becoming popular throughout Europe.

Fishing

For many years the coasts of southern and western Spain were very poor. People from villages by the sea made a living by catching fish. In the last thirty years some of these fishing villages, such as Fuengirola and Benidorm, have become popular tourist resorts, but some fishing continues. On the Atlantic coast of the north-west, fishing is an important industry. Special refrigerated trains carry the fish overnight to the big cities, so there is always fresh fish available in Madrid first thing in the morning.

Above *Benidorm, on the Costa Blanca, was once a small fishing village but has now become a busy tourist resort full of huge skyscrapers.*

Left *An old fishing village on the Costa Blanca.*

Cooking ingredients

Above *Some nearly ripe olives.*

Olive oil is one of the most important ingredients in Spanish cookery. The oil is made by crushing and pressing the olives. Olives are also a popular cooking ingredient, and people often eat them as *tapas*, or snacks. Olives that are to be eaten are usually picked green and then cured. Black olives are the ones that have been left on the tree to ripen; olive oil is usually made from black olives.

Spanish onions are famous throughout the world. Many Spanish recipes begin with frying onions or garlic, or both, in

Right *Garlic for sale at an open-air market.*

olive oil. In southern Spain, people often like to have garlic, salt and olive oil on their toast.

Chorizo is a special type of cured sausage made from pork. It is very tasty and may be eaten on its own, but it is very good when added to a stew. Ham is also used in stews and eaten as a *tapa*. Most bars and households have a leg of ham hanging up in the kitchen. Spanish ham is specially cured, giving it a strong flavour and chewy texture.

Above Chorizo, *a popular Spanish sausage, hanging up in a butcher's shop.*

Left *An early morning delivery of freshly baked bread.*

Spanish bread is very tasty, and its cake-like texture makes it very filling. Most families buy fresh bread from the bakery every day.

Sweet peppers, carrots, potatoes and tomatoes are the favourite vegetables for making stews. Usually two or three different types of vegetables are cooked together in olive oil. In addition to vegetables, a stew may be made with meat, lentils, chickpeas or beans.

Spanish cheese is usually quite hard and can have a very strong flavour. The most popular cheese is called Manchego cheese because it comes from the region of La Mancha. It is made from sheep's milk. Cheese is not used much in Spanish cooking, but is a popular *tapa*.

Saffron is made by collecting and drying the tiny orange-coloured stigmas inside the petals of a crocus. It has a strong bitter flavour and makes the food it is cooked with yellow. Saffron is used in stews and in a rice dish called *paella*.

This man is picking the flowers of saffron crocus. The orange-red stigmas are removed from the flower and dried to produce saffron threads.

Meal times

Spaniards love to spend a long time eating large meals. Almost everyone drinks wine with their meals, including the children, who are given a little wine mixed with water.

Traditionally, *la comida* (lunch) is the most important meal of the day. It is

A Spanish family enjoying la comida.

23

eaten in the middle of the afternoon, at about 2 or 3 o'clock, and often the whole family, including young children and grandparents who live nearby, eat together. *La comida* usually includes vegetables, fish, meat and pudding. After the meal most people have a *siesta*, or nap, for an hour or so. Some lucky people do not have to go back to work after lunch, but there is school in the afternoons. Spanish children do not have a 'bedtime' and often stay up as late as their parents. They do not get tired or sleepy because they have had a *siesta* after their late lunch.

In the big cities, like Madrid and Barcelona, people usually work or go to school too far away to come home for *la comida*. For these families, *la cena* (supper), rather than lunch, becomes the main meal. In more traditional places, like Seville, *la cena* is a small meal. It may be just a sandwich made with tasty bread; this is called a *bocadillo*, which means 'mouthful'. Many people do not bother with supper; instead, the whole family goes out to eat *tapas* (see page 26).

People having a snack at an open-air café in Madrid.

For breakfast, adults may have a cup of coffee and some toast in a bar on their way to work. Children may have some fruit juice and take a *bocadillo* to school to eat during break time. But almost everyone likes to have *churros* for breakfast once in a while. They are like deep-fried doughnuts in the shape of giant bendy pencils. The best way to eat a *churro* is to dip it into a thick, sweet hot chocolate.

At about six o'clock in the evening is *merienda*, or tea time. People usually drink hot chocolate or coffee rather than tea. *Merienda* is never complete without a rich cake or pastry.

Churro, *a spiral doughnut, is a favourite treat for most Spaniards.*

Tapas

During the day most bars and cafés serve small snacks called *tapas*. The word *tapa* means 'lid', and some people say that *tapas* were originally small pieces of bread that were placed on top of a drink to stop flies from falling into it. The bar owners then added other foods to these pieces of bread in order to attract more customers. When people began to go to bars especially to eat *tapas*, the bar owners stopped giving them away free. In some places, bar owners still give a few peanuts or a bowl

A variety of tapas *on display in a* tapas *bar.*

of olives free with a drink, but normally you have to pay extra for a *tapa*.

Nowadays people sometimes eat a few different *tapas* instead of having lunch. But people usually eat *tapas* at about 12 o'clock so that they do not get too hungry waiting for their late lunch. Having *tapas* is always a good time to meet with friends. Sometimes people gather in big groups and eat their *tapas* standing up. A good *tapas* bar is always very noisy. It is considered polite to order extra *tapas* for your friends, even when they say no.

The typical *tapas* served in most bars are fried prawns, potato omelette, *ensaladilla* (see the recipe on page 36) and olives. There are other special *tapas* that vary from region to region. Most places near the sea have plenty of fish and shellfish, sardines, anchovies, mussels and clams for *tapas*. Further away from the sea, people often eat slices of ham and spicy *chorizos*.

A busy tapas *bar in Barcelona.*

Fiestas

It is said that you can find a *fiesta*, or festival, somewhere in Spain every day of the year. Some *fiestas* can last for days and they usually include processions, and dancing and singing in the streets. Traditional *fiesta* foods are *turrón*, a kind of chocolate nougat, and *yemas*, egg yolks boiled in syrup.

Turrón, *a traditional festive food, is made with honey, sugar, chocolate, nuts and dried fruit.*

Most Spaniards are very religious, and the Roman Catholic religion is an important part of most *fiestas*. Each town has its own special *fiesta* in honour of its patron saint, who looks after the town and its people.

The most important fiesta is *Semana Santa*, the Holy Week leading up to Easter. The *Semana Santa* celebrations in Seville are world famous. Every day and night, during the week-long celebrations, statues of the Virgin Mary and Jesus are carried through the streets. Thousands of people wearing special costumes walk in front and behind, carrying candles, while brass bands play.

A Holy Week procession carrying a statue of the Virgin Mary.

According to legend, Santiago (St James), the patron saint of Spain, is buried at the church of Santiago de Compostela in Galicia. This is the holiest shrine in Spain, visited by pilgrims from all over Spain and the rest of the world. Every seven years is called the year of St James. During this special year millions of pilgrims – including the Pope – visit the shrine.

Santiago de Compostela, the shrine of St James, is visited by thousands of pilgrims every year.

A taste of Spain

These giant figures built for Las Fallas *will be set alight on the last night of this three-day* fiesta.

At the end of March there is *Las Fallas* in Valencia. Groups of people spend all year and a great deal of money making huge models of various people or things. Some models can be more than thirty metres high. During *Las Fallas*, the models are put on show in the main squares of the city for three days and nights. On the third night they are set on fire and there is a fireworks display.

One *fiesta* in Alicante can get rather messy. At midday trucks arrive full of tomatoes and there is an enormous tomato fight that lasts for over an hour. Those who wish to avoid tomato stains stay at home; the rest wear old clothes.

Regional specialities

Cooking traditions and eating habits vary greatly among the seventeen regions of Spain. This means that there are many regional specialities.

Zarzuela de pescado is a speciality in Catalonia. *Zarzuela* is the Spanish word for a musical or an operetta, and *pescado* is the word for fish. This 'musical fish' dish is made by cooking a variety of shellfish in white wine.

Paella *is a rice dish made with a variety of different ingredients, depending on what is available. It is cooked in a large two-handled pan, which is also called a* paella.

A taste of Spain

Valencia is the home of the famous *paella*. The basic ingredient is rice, which is cooked with a variety of foods including shellfish, fish, vegetables and sometimes meat. The word *paella* comes from the Roman word for a pan. It was the Romans who brought rice to Spain, and this rice dish is cooked in a special pan, also called a *paella*, which is large and shallow.

In Aragon people eat meat cooked in a *chilindron* sauce, which is made of sweet red peppers, garlic and tomatoes.

Red chilli peppers drying in the sun. The dried peppers are used for colouring and flavouring chorizos *and sauces.*

The Basques are famous sea-fishermen, and *Bacalao al pil-pil* is a typical dish from the Basque Country. Nowadays *bacalao* is a slang word for 'house-music', but it really means 'cod'. *Pil-pil*

is a type of sauce made with chilli peppers, garlic and oil.

Navarre is well known for its river-fish, especially trout.

Asturias is home of the *fabada*. This is a delicious stew made with *fabades* (white beans), ham bone, bacon and *morcilla* (black pudding). It is especially good on a cold winter's day.

Galicia is best known for its seafood dishes, which the Galicians like to eat with a local wine called Ribeiro.

Madrid is famed for *cocido*, a type of stew served in two parts: first the stew is strained and the broth is served on its own; the rest of the stew – a mixture of chickpeas, chicken and vegetables – is served afterwards.

Pisto Manchego from La Mancha is a fried vegetable dish that has become a popular dish throughout Spain. La Mancha is also famous for something other than food. Don Quixote and Sancho Panza, two characters from Spain's most famous novel, written by Miguel de Cervantes, came from La Mancha.

In Andalusia the regional speciality is *huevos a la flamenca*, which means 'flamenco eggs'. It is a delicious stew topped with eggs and baked in the oven. Flamenco refers to a type of dance that comes from that area. The most famous dish from Andalusia is *gazpacho* (see the recipe on page 34), a refreshing soup that is usually served in the summer.

Above *A small farm in Asturias on the north Atlantic coast.*

Above *Miguel de Cervantes and his fictional characters.*
Below *Huevos a la flamenca.*

33

Gazpacho Andaluz

Ingredients
Serves 4 to 6

4 giant tomatoes
1 green pepper
1 cucumber
2 cloves of garlic
1–2 handfuls of stale
   bread crumbs
5 tablespoons of
   olive oil
water
vinegar
salt
pepper

Equipment

knife
chopping board
garlic crusher
liquidizer
large mixing bowl

Gazpacho is a famous cold soup from Andalusia in southern Spain.

Before peeling the tomatoes, first place them in a saucepan of boiling water for about half a minute, strain them and pour cold water over them. Now the skins will come off very easily.

1 Peel the tomatoes. Cut off the stalk of the pepper and clean out the seeds. Chop the tomatoes, pepper and cucumber into small pieces. Crush the garlic.

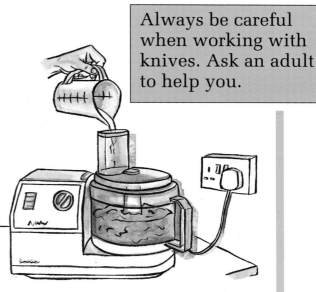

Always be careful when working with knives. Ask an adult to help you.

2 Liquidize the chopped vegetables and the garlic.

4 Stir in about a litre of water, a little bit at a time. Meanwhile season with salt and pepper and a few dashes of vinegar. Keep tasting the soup while you do this. When you think it has the right consistency and flavour, the soup is ready.

3 Add the bread crumbs and oil to the vegetable mixture. Liquidize the mixture again.

5 Keep the soup in the fridge and serve it cold.

Ensaladilla

Ingredients

Serves 4 to 6

4 large potatoes
2 medium-sized
   carrots
2 eggs
2 handfuls of olives
   without stones
3 sweet red peppers
250 g tuna fish
350 g mayonnaise
water

Equipment

knife
chopping board
2 saucepans
large shallow bowl

Ensaladilla is a type of salad that is very popular as a *tapa* or as a first course.

Sweet red peppers and carrots for sale at an outdoor market.

Always be careful when working with knives. Ask an adult to help you.

3   Chop the olives into small pieces.

1   Peel the potatoes and cut them into small pieces. Wash the carrots and dice them. Put the carrots and potatoes in a saucepan of water, bring to the boil and simmer for about 15 minutes. Drain the water from the potatoes and carrots and leave them to cool.

4   Cut the stalks from the peppers and clean out the seeds. Then cut the peppers into small pieces.

5   Put the carrots, potatoes, peppers, olives, tuna fish, the chopped egg and most of the mayonnaise together in a shallow bowl and mix them well.

2   While the vegetables are cooking, hard boil the eggs by putting them in boiling water for about 10 minutes. Let the eggs cool down, then peel them. Chop one of the eggs into very small pieces; cut the other into slices.

6   Flatten down the top of the *ensaladilla* and spread the rest of the mayonnaise in a thin layer over the top. Decorate the top with the egg slices. Keep it in the fridge until you are ready to serve it.

Pan con tomate y jamon

(Bread with tomatoes and ham)

This snack from Catalonia is quick and easy to prepare.

Ingredients

Serves 4 to 6

1 stick of french bread
(or a loaf of freshly
baked white bread)
2 ripe tomatoes
olive oil
salt
a few slices of ham

Equipment

knife
chopping board

This man is holding a jabuga ham, which is made from pigs that have been fed on acorns. The meat is taken high up into the mountains and cured in the open air.

1 Cut the bread into slices (about 2 cm thick).

2 Cut the tomatoes in half.

3 Rub the tomatoes on the slices of bread. Try to leave as much of the flesh of the tomatoes as possible on the bread.

4 Pour a little olive oil on to each slice of bread and season with salt.

5 Put a piece of ham on top of each slice of bread.

Always be careful when working with knives. Ask an adult to help you.

Horchata

Ingredients
Serves 2

200 g tiger nuts
125 g sugar
1 l of water

Equipment

saucepan
liquidizer
bowl
sieve
wooden spoon

Horchata is a very refreshing drink that is served all over Spain. Nowadays it often comes in a bottle, but it is much better when freshly made.

You can buy tiger nuts in a health food shop. For this recipe, you need to soak the tiger nuts in water overnight. Then rinse them well.

1 Heat the water, but do not let it boil.

Always be careful when heating up water. Ask an adult to help you.

2 Put the tiger nuts and the hot water into the liquidizer and blend them until you have a smooth mixture.

3 Press the mixture through the sieve with a wooden spoon.

4 Add the sugar to the mixture and stir it in well.

5 Leave to cool and then chill the *horchata* in the fridge for about 4 hours before serving.

Empanada Gallega

(Galician pasty)

A harbour scene in Galicia.

Pan means 'bread' in Spanish, and *empanada* means 'breaded'. *Empanada Gallega* is half way between a pie and a pasty.

Ingredients

Serves 4

1 medium-sized
  onion
olive oil
flour
225 g puff pastry
185 g tuna fish, in
  chunks
paprika and salt
1 egg

Equipment

knife
chopping board
frying pan
wooden spoon
rolling pin
baking tray
bowl
fork
oven gloves

1 Peel and chop the onion.

2 Heat a tablespoon of the oil in the frying pan. Fry the onion, stirring it from time to time with a wooden spoon, until it begins to turn golden brown (about 5 minutes). Take it off the heat.

Be careful when heating the oil and chopping the onion. Ask an adult to help you.

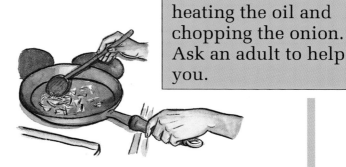

3 Sprinkle a little flour on a clean surface and rub some on to the rolling pin. Roll out the pastry. You want to end up with the pastry in two squares, one the same size as the base of the baking tray, and the other slightly larger.

4 Put a little oil on to the baking tray and smear it around until the bottom is covered.

5 Lay the larger piece of pastry neatly on to the baking tray. Smear a little oil over the top of the pastry.

6 Spread the onion and the chunks of tuna fish on top of the pastry. Season with a little paprika and salt.

7 Crack the egg into a bowl and beat well with a fork.

8 Put the second piece of pastry over the top. Pinch the edges of the two pieces of pastry together so that you have a closed pocket. Make sure you do not leave any gaps in the pastry. Brush the beaten egg over the pastry.

9 Bake the *empanada* in a pre-heated oven, set at 200°C or gas mark 6, for 25 minutes. Let it cool slightly before serving.

Glossary

Ancestors People from whom we are descended, such as grandparents.

Ancient Belonging to times long past.

Aqueduct A canal that is built to carry water from one area to another.

Archaeologist A person who studies ancient cultures by digging up ancient cities, buildings or artefacts.

Capital The city that is the seat of the country's government.

Celts An ancient people from central and western Europe.

Citrus fruit A type of slightly acidic fruit covered with thick skin that grows on trees or shrubs in warm climates. Oranges, lemons, limes and grapefruits are all citrus fruits.

Civil War A war between citizens of the same country.

Conquer To gain control, usually by force, over another group of people.

Cured When referring to food, cured means the food has been smoked or salted to preserve it or to improve the flavour.

Democratic government A system of government in which the people hold the power through elected representatives.

Dialect A variation of a spoken language that is commonly used by a particular group of people.

Dictator A ruler who has complete power and authority over all the people in the country.

Empire A group of countries under the control of another country.

Explorers People who travel to an unknown territory to learn about the land and its people.

Export To sell goods to another country.

Iberian Peninsula The peninsula in south-west Europe occupied by Spain and Portugal.

Irrigation Supplying land with water, using a system of channels, ditches or aqueducts.

Muslims Followers of the religion of Islam and the Prophet Mohammed.

Patron saint A saint that is looked upon as a special guardian of a person or place.

Peninsula A piece of land that juts out into the sea and is almost completely surrounded by water (from the Latin meaning 'almost an island').

Pilgrim A person who makes a trip, or a pilgrimage, to a church, shrine or some other holy place that is important to his or her religion.

Roman Catholic religion A Christian religion. The head of the Roman Catholic Church is the Pope.

Romans People from Rome, Italy. About 2,000 years ago, the ancient Romans ruled over most of Europe and parts of Africa and the Middle East.

Shrine A sacred or holy place.

Stigmas The parts of a flower that receive pollen grains from another plant, which in turn allows a seed to form.

Terrace A series of flat platforms of earth, rising one above the other on the side of a hill.

Traditional A way of doing something that has not changed for years.

Visigoths A branch of the Goths who came from present-day Germany. They invaded the Roman Empire late in the fourth century AD and eventually set up a kingdom in Spain.

Picture acknowledgements

The publishers would like to thank the following for allowing their photographs to be reproduced: Anthony Blake Photo Library 21 top, 25, 26, 33 bottom, 34 (all by Gerrit Buntrock); Chapel Studios: Zul cover inset, 40; Eye Ubiquitous 16 bottom (Mike Southern); Cephas Picture Library 17, 18 top, 20 bottom (all by Mick Rock), 28 (Roy Stedell); J Allan Cash 7, 8 top, 10 bottom, 12, 14 both, 15, 16 top, 19 bottom, 38; Greg Evans International Picture Library 10 top, 42 (Benn Keaveney); Explorer 27 bottom (H. Donnezar); Bob Goodwin 21 bottom; Robert Harding Picture Library 9, 23, 30 (Robert Frerck); Anthony King 13, 22, 32, 33 top; Tony Stone Worldwide cover (Oliver Benn), frontispiece (Tony Caddock), 4 (Robert Frerck), 6 (Tony Craddock), 8 bottom (Manfred Mehlig), 18 bottom (Robert Frerck), 19 top (Alan Smith), 24 (Doug Armand), 29 top (Thomas Ennis), 29 bottom (John Bradley), 36 (Val Corbett); Wayland Picture Library 20 top, 31, 33 middle; Zefa 11.

The map artwork on page 5 was supplied by Peter Bull. The recipe artwork on pages 34 to 44 was supplied by Judy Stevens.

Further information

Books to read

Catalan Cuisine by Colman
Andrews (Headline, 1988)

Food around the World by
Ridgwell and Ridgway
(Oxford University Press,
1986)

*Recipes from a Spanish
Village* by Pepita Aris
(Conran Octopus, 1990)

Spain by Manuel Avarado
(Wayland, 1989)

Spanish Food and Drink by
Maria Eugenia D. Pellicer
(Wayland, 1987)

The Flavours of Andalusia by
Elizabeth Luard (Colins and
Brown, 1991)

Useful addresses

Foods from Spain
Spanish Embassy
Commercial Office
Chiltern Street
London W1

('Foods from Spain' promotes
Spanish food in Britain.)

Cervantes Institute
169 Woodhouse Lane,
Leeds, Yorkshire LS2 3AR

Cervantes Institute
102 Eaton Square,
London SW1W 9AN

(The Cervantes Institute
promotes Spanish culture.)

Acknowledgements
The authors wish to thank Michael Jacobs, Elena Horas and Godfrey and Gillian Goodwin
for their assistance and advice.

Index